CL!T

I0081484

cunning linguist tome

Richard "Shake" White

Released November 2023

Printed in the United States of America
Photography Mad-Imagery
Cover Design Christopher Michael
Edited By Sunni Soper
ISBN 979-8-9880540-3-0
Published by 310 Brown Street
www.310brownstreet.com
www.mrmichael310.com

Richard "Shake" White

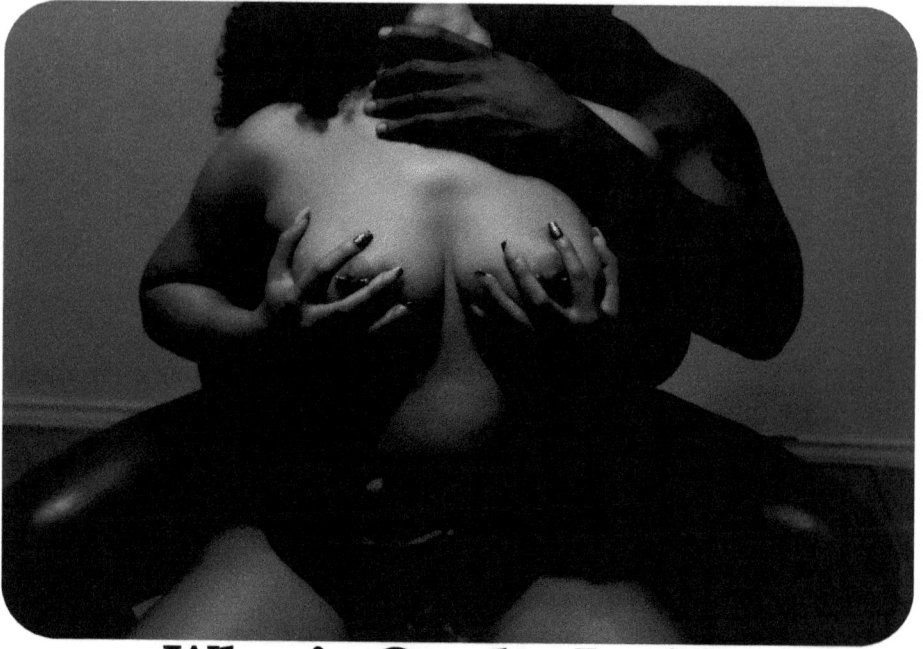

What's On the Inside

Chapter 1: Softer

Chapter 2: Harder

Chapter 3: Deeper

Richard "Shake" White

SOFT

Richard "Shake" White

Before our second session...
You be the Director
Provide direction, make corrections
Until the sexing is pure perfection and nothing less than
Orgasms after orgasms of yours, ours
Floors, showers
Lost track...
Yet we've devoured four hours
I'll go down til the Sun comes up
Just a preview to this Full-length Feature...
Film us for future reference
Prepare me to be your preference
A perfectly presented presentation
Tongue tingling, touching, tasting
Wanting, waiting in anticipation
Cunnilingus and coitus, call her to cum join us
And point us in the right direction
Navigate me as I explore you, I implore you
There's more you to become acquainted
Picture us how you want it and I will paint it
Stroking you North, South
Holding open your throat, mouth
Palming your scalp, gripping your strands
Or braiding our fingers, clenching your hands
Just guide me, ride me
Suffocate these lips between your hips and thighs
Make temperatures rise
Squeeze, I don't need to breathe
Just create scenes that dreams get wet from
I will wade and wallow
Play any position I'm given, ready to follow
Let's point and shoot, aim to please
Beasts unleashed, let me tame and ease
Let's record and revisit
Make so many revisions and reminders
That I can find it blinded, with my hands binded, bound
In the absence of sound

Cause by taste and smell, I can tell it's you
Don't just tell me, show me
Teach me about your body, I want to learn slowly... Precision
I need to know in each position and how you function, seduction
Define and describe your desires between touching and fucking
I'm searching for knowledge, head...
Aches and pains in our backs and legs
Take your time and I'll give you mine
Running my fingers along your ribs and spine
Lips massaging every stretch mark, every scar
Until I've tasted your spirit, mind, body, and heart
Be your comforter beneath the comforters
Tell me how you like it, I will scribe it in the sheets
Keep you covered in these covers, I will read all in-between
Say what you mean
I mean orchestrate our orgasms
Maybe manage a menage
Tell me to get lost and found in it
That you want me pounding it
Hold me down until I drown in it
Have your body invite me in, welcome and accept me
I love to hunt, but I'd rather you just say what you want
...Directly

Richard "Shake" White

Foot Rubs in the Park

Let's go drive and park by a small body of water
And never get out the car
Stay there until the Sun disappears from the sky
And we're only left with the stars
Sit back, put your feet in my lap, relax while I give a massage
I'm craving for that time alone, a ménage
When it be just you with me and God
Tell me about your day, even the things you think nobody wants to
hear of
Getting closer to your heart, the part I want to take care of
I'm listening because I care Love
Caressing the stress out of your soles
My lips and tongue begin massaging your toes
Fingertips tenderly treading your tendons
Palms securing your ankles
I'm here to thank you
For the work you've done, miles you've walked
Talk to me
I still find your dreams and aspirations fascinating
Your every accomplishment I'm congratulating
Let it out when you pout about procrastinating
Or whatever has been aggravating you
I'm here for that conversation
Exchanging unrehearsed verses of our versions is enough of a sermon
to be of service
Admittingly, I've never been this nervous about Churching
Your presence perfect...
And I love being in it
Hate when it's ended
Some say "Don't start what you can't finish"
So as every passing minute is diminished
I'm trying to make these few hours ours
Shower you with compliments, give you your flowers
A Rose is still a rose
I could bask in that bush, pluck on your petals
Embrace every thorn, never escape or run from your perils

11

Looking at life behind your eyes, staring down both barrels
I feel at home here... Safe
There's never been a better place than you and I sharing the same space
I want to be face to face, gripping your hips, kissing your lips
Tasting your secrets before you speak them
I seek them, promise to never leak them
I see them as bridges from your thoughts to mine
Connecting soul, body, and mind
Until we're close enough for your sweat to rehydrate my skin on contact
On contact... I begin to feel the butterflies inside
So, I'm not surprised that I just want to cocoon with you and just bloom
And whatever that last thought was, you can tell me about that too
For me... this is all about you

Richard "Shake" White

Shhh...
Come and sit with me, I'm listening
Remembering the rhythm of your heart's beat
Take a seat
Hand me your feet
And I'll massage your soul through your soles
Don't moan a peep
Deep sleep, fall if you'd like,
We've got all life to spend nights
I'm just trying to hear you right
Shhh...
I'm still learning the language of your soul
How to speak to your secrets and Braille your body
Paying attention to every mention of how to love you properly
From navigating away from the tales that broke you
To knowing when to grab you by throat and choke you as I stroke you
I want to know you... On that ethereal level
I want to learn the seasonings your momma put in your baby-food
Hear the tunes that made your hips move, your toes tap and lips whistle
This'll be the greatest song ever sung
I want to hear what your heart heard when it realized my heart knew she was the one
Shhh...
Come closer for a second
Just enough to feel my passion upon your neck
As intensely as our bodies clashing when we're naked
Let me taste your truth, savor your history
Let me provide safe haven, escape from your misery
Taste you spiritually, touch you mentally, and fuck you physically
I just want to ravage that body viciously while I handle you sensually
Cosmically, chemically, it'll always feel like it's meant to be
There you go being loud again
Shhh...
Don't make a sound, there's no need to utter a word
I've already heard what you would have said
Just lie back and spread, I've been waiting to be fed
It's time for your inner thighs to be more acquainted with my head

Lips to labia, vibrating the vulva, creating connections with your clit
While you're still trying to get naked
Starving, I couldn't wait for you to strip
Teasing the tip with your fingertips gripping
Beckoning my body to put you into position
To have our hips kissing
Shhh…
Listen

Richard "Shake" White

Richard "Shake" White

The Invitation

She said, "Come in, the waters' fine"...
I had no reason to decline the invitation
I had been waiting for this
Been patient for this, been aching to kiss,
Tongue tracing the tats on her back
Fucking the bubbles out of the bath, squeezing that ass tighter, the tighter she gripped me
Slippery when wet...
Longing to know just how nasty she can get
She's thick and I'm starving
I hardened at the thought
I've been feigning to have her creaming
And I thought I was dreaming
Until the smell of candles and potpourri awoken me
Envisioning her lips stroking me, my tip probing
I've been hoping and waiting for just a taste
Craving her touch, her plush, making her blush
By the way this lust is making my blood rush
I could tell that this was one hell of a crush...
So, I stood there, in awe
Mentally making love to every part of her that I saw
Her beauty and nudity had me consumed
She invited me into the room, the bed
She began with head... Then tail
We battled for position until we prevailed
When she came, she rained and hailed
I stood in the storm catching raindrops, face drenched
Without letting go, waist clenched
A mess to clean
I'd been wanting to kneel and bow ever since I met the Queen
I began to tidy a bit with my lips hiding her clit
No denying, her hips kept my head in place while she was riding my face
I had to taste her energy as she lost it...
Somehow remaining at my hardest, while deep within her softness
She moaned, "Cum, get lost in it"
Me wanting to turn and toss in it

17

I was happy to oblige
But first use these hands to secure, my tongue to massage
Cause if this was the last time, I had to make time last
Taking the candles from around the tub to rub the wax into the small of her back
Running my fingers through her scalp and gripping while kissing her collarbone and neck
Sucking on her breasts, nipples erect as I
She said, "Come in, the waters fine"...
And though we had fucked many times in my mind
I thought to myself, "It's about damn time"

Richard "Shake" White

Take My Time

I know...
Take my time, do it slow
You've been walking all day let me suck those toes...
Lick up your calves till I reach your ass,
Eat your ass after I've splashed my face in your sweetest place
I've been longing to taste you
Lay you down, lift you up
I didn't come here to fuck,
But no part of you will be left untouched
Suck... On your inner thighs, breasts and neck
Discover spots on you that no man has visited yet
Stretch... More than your imagination
Show you that 'loving the fuck out of you' was no exaggeration
Following your commands better than your own hands during masturbation
Bodies clapping more like "Congratulating"
There maybe a little untying,
A lot of sweating and crying,
I am trying to be prying your mind from your matter
Fingers motioning your orgasms towards me
Left hand applying pressure to your bladder
Using both hands to make sure everything is eaten off of this platter
I've been longing to please you
I've been wanting to tease you
Now that I'm here with you
I'm going to eat you, feed you and read you
Cover to cover
Believe me, I'm leaving smothered... drenched
This fire burning inside me needs to be quenched
Quieted, quelled
Your body shall be held and inhaled
For its touch, taste, and smell
Diving into your well
Keeping you constantly coming... Out of your shell
Stimulating your senses
Kisses in abundance
Listening to how you want it

Until you more than feel me in your stomach...
With you, I plan to get deep enough to find something to believe in
Leaving palm prints on the surfaces of everywhere that we've been
Taking you over the deep end
Back of your legs where the knees bend
We've been neglecting a few areas haven't we
Aren't you curious
Reaching for new heights tonight, it's all about appetite
I know it's tight and luxurious
I've got cravings and a sweet tooth to satisfy
To you, with you, for you, I'll do more than pacify
Anything that I'm forgetting, just ask and I...
Will bring into fruition
There's nowhere I wouldn't take you, or be afraid to go
I know...
Take my time, do it slow...

Richard "Shake" White

How about, you and me in the room, nothing on but the music, spooning,
creating our own acoustics
Melodically erotic, two bodies…one rhythm, one harmony…
same tone - we stay tuned - into the station
of penetration, sensations, skin tasting, lips parted to speak to where hips part –
they meet and greet and share the sweetest of secrets. Thighs hug around my lungs,
you're conducting the fucking anyway you want it, loving the way I touch it, rub it, just right,
you be-flat… lay on your back. I orchestrate orgasms that come from middle C….
Sexual symphony, simply sing for me when your strings are strummed, come til your knees spring like Piano keys: No rushing, but we're lusting for percussion,
heartbeats like snares, pulling your hair. Your lips smack to grip Sax, as your vocal cords
record like they've never recorded before…performed like you choreographed this
Score… I find bass, my face placed at your hips and waist. I taste your soul…
all night we rock and baby we roll,
Lose control of our emotions, spoken words never heard or mentioned.
We switch positions by nature's intentions
We're listening, loving the music we make as we lay….
Hold that note in the back of your throat…Let's choke on this song we wrote,
don't change the tempo, let's crescendo, increase the intensity, the energy.
Sing from your diaphragm, let the world hear what I've composed while doors were closed.
Let's sing into the mezzanine, let's be seen as King and Queen in an Opera,
as I ignite your chakras, Shake in my hands like Maracas, and listen…

to the sound of us breathing - and moaning. We're flowing in the perfect verse as if we rehearsed it first.

No chorus for us to play, an endless rhyme…bend your spine… Sing into the Heavens,

Deafen me…sexually, body satisfied, mind pacified, touch magnified til sensory senses start slipping slowly….

hold me… like I'm your last note, breathe life into my instrument…when you blow (don't-let-go)

Body facing me, gracefully keeping pace with me. Faithfully waiting patiently- un hastily.

You're tasting me as I leave your hips….

This key signature is perfect…

When my tongue scribbles in cursive…

I heard it, and our musical…

sounds so Beautiful

Arms around a Harp held next to my heart,

this is art…

Let's write sheet music in the sheets and sleep to our own beat after I've synthesized the fire in my eyes with the passion in your thighs.

Let's rewind at sunrise,

Apple of my eye,

you can be my student

Making love is a must,

but I wanna teach you

How to make music

*Courtesy of previously published works written by Shake the poet (Richard White)

Parts of you I've never seen

Parts of you I've never seen
When our lips met
I feared being misled...
You sat on the edge of the bed, hips spread
And your grip said, everything I wanted to hear
It was clear
You wanted to be there as much as I wanted you near
Once our lips parted I started becoming an Artist perfecting his craft
Hands molding, caressing your ass
Tongue running up your calves and learning how bad you wanted to
be grabbed
I took my time getting to know you
I didn't mind trying to show you
Just how long I've been longing to answer your body's calling
I mean... I've seen so vividly in my dreams
Parts of you I'd never seen
Heard you moan and scream, you creamed and came
I did the same and we became waves
Fingers... Became braids as our fists clenched each other
Bodies kissed each other
We fit, like we had missed each other
Didn't have to teach each other, foreign yet familiar
I'd gotten lost in your eyes, so soft
Gripping your thighs when you were riding
I could see myself inside them
Held tightly, but she began to widen to fit me
Passionately, the way my love filled you
Made you forget what it felt like to feel empty
It was as if I practiced cunnilingual calligraphy
The way my tongue wrote scriptures across your clitoris
You began to babble my name
We became like candle and flame
You engulfed the tip, just to dance on the wick
Though nothing left to strip, sweat dripped
Pressed lips on skin
You beckoned, "Again?!?"

23

I was happy to oblige
You opened wide and took me inside
Climbed, scaled, and mounted me
Divided your time between crowning and drowning me
Headboard pounding the walls
While I pounded yours
Finding you on all fours
Backdoor, I began to explore
Tongue and thumb in
You coming, cum running
Both of our 5 senses were summoned, this type of loving
Doesn't come a dime a dozen
So sexually satisfied, you couldn't remember the last time you wasn't
Hearts pumping, blood rushing from our touching and tasting
Curing cravings
I just laid there in amazement
Head Doctor and Patient
Embracing your waist while giving face
Give and take
You caved in and gave in, taking every inch of me
Engraving my name into your DNA so deeply you begin to shake
whenever somebody mentions me
We were completely nude, utterly naked, exposed
I saw so much of the real you I could feel you
I wanted every bit of that...
And I still do

Richard "Shake" White

The Interviews (#1)

Describe your sexual preference/orientation (ex. Bi, Poly, etc)
I am most definitely Bi-sexual.
Do you prefer sensuality over physicality? (love making or fucking) explain?
Definitely fucking! They'd have to be somebody I really like for me to be sensual.
What is the easiest way to turn you on / what turns you off?
Touching and kissing my neck turns me the hell on. Turnoffs are definitely the way they talk. Fuck my brain 1st! or it won't work for me.
Describe an ideal sexual encounter with you.
Fucking! I'm gonna tell you what I like so we ain't gotta waste time. Let's cut to the business.
How do you perform cunnilingus/fellatio? (give tips and tricks)
I actually give great head. No gag reflex, breathe through your nose, relax your throat. You have to enjoy doing it. I don't mind asking what they like etc. I watched a lot of porn to learn how to give head so, lol.
How do you like oral to be performed on you? (give tips and tricks)
I'm actually not a big head person. I don't like when people suck on me, or to be licked like a cat. Nibble the clit, have some type of motion with the tongue. Don't be a pussy while eating the pussy.
How do you feel about anal? (oral, penetration, toys etc)
I have a 2-finger limit. No penis in the butt. I'm cool with eating ass, but not too much penetration for me.
How do you feel about bondage? (ever tried it)
I've never really tried it, but I like rough sex, so I guess I would like it. I like being choked and stuff.
What are your thoughts on Role Play? What would be an ideal RP?
I'm terrible with roleplay, it gets awkward. I like dirty talk, but like I said…let's get to work. I prefer to be your little slut.
Favorite position(s) and why?
From the back of course, cause my arch game is on point.

What is so special about sexual intercourse with you?

I've been told that I have great vagina. I'm not the average girl who wants to be lovey dovey... I've been told I'm like a nigga. I'm very direct

Masturbation: How often, what do you do/use?

I believe a nut a day keeps the doctor away. It's good for your mental health, instead of going out looking for penis. Clitoral stimulation is my thing.

What do you desire to be done to you?

I like to be played with, nipples sucked on, choked, spanked and told what to do. Being a sex slave is a lot of fun.

What's the wildest thing you've ever done or were asked to do sexually?

The wildest thing that happened to me was someone accidentally tried to get in my butt, lol.

What are your thoughts on 3-somes/orgies?

I'm down, I think they're fun. They're fun when everybody is down.

Have you ever participated in a 3-some/orgy? How was it? Would you do it again?

Yes, Yes I would do it again, they are fun

What could be improved about your 3-some/orgy experience?

Nothing really. As long as everyone is comfortable with it.

What do you think about casual sex between acquaintances/friends?

That's me all the time because I hate boyfriends. I don't have the time. So, I like to find a good fuckbuddy and call it a day.

What signs do you give off to let someone know that 'they can get it'?

I just tell them ...what's up, are we fucking or nah?

How would you like to be asked/propositioned for a sexual encounter?

Don't beat around the bush. If you're getting that energy from me, speak up...we can correct it if we're wrong.

How much does size matter to you? (Total Body ie stomach, breast, booty, lips, penis, clit etc)

So, I like big boys... but I don't really have a type. Penis size matters, it can't be tiny, I need something to work with, but I don't want a GIANT penis...there is a "too big" thing. I like boobs...

I like thicker people... I don't think giant fake boobs are cute, I like real people.

Bonus: What is your advice that wasn't covered in the questions asked?

Be vocal, be upfront and communicate your wants, desires etc. Like I said no beating around the bush.

The Interviews (2)

Describe your sexual preference/orientation (ex. Bi, Poly, etc)

Bisexual/poly I like men and women and have multiple partners

Do you prefer sensuality over physicality? (love making or fucking) explain?

Depends on the person. I can be intimate and sensual with a woman, but with a Man I prefer to be fucked.

What is the easiest way to turn you on / what turns you off?

Mental stimulation, sucking on my titties! Turn offs, smells, cocky attitude, toxicity, expecting to go straight to town. When receiving head and the person is inexperienced, I prefer nice and nasty.

Describe an ideal sexual encounter with you

On the beach... walking on the beach and I want someone to take over. I don't want to think, I want them to make me forget where I'm at in the most intimate and nasty way.

How do you perform cunnilingus/fellatio? (give tips and tricks)

Cunnilingus: very sensual, I start by kissing on her lips, move to her neck and start grabbing and scratching on her back. I then kiss all the way down to her pussy, I then go in... I reach up and play with her titties, then go back up and let her taste herself on my lips and repeat.

Fellatio: I let them take over, I prefer my men to be in control in the bedroom. If they don't know what to do, I pretty much do the same I that I do with women. But I like to ride too so I have to jump on that thing in between the head session.

How do you like oral to be performed on you? (give tips and tricks)

I like a nice and slow rhythmic, little sloppy, circular, with a lot of sucking on the clit, as if you were massaging my clit with your tongue and lips

How do you feel about anal? (oral, penetration, toys etc)

I've only received oral, and I'm not sure if I am open to being penetrated anally. But the oral feels amazing.

How do you feel about bondage? (ever tried it)

Yes. I have been tied up. I like it and want to learn more about it. I've handcuffed a partner before. I'm really into 50 shades. I plan to incorporate more of that in the future.

What are your thoughts on Role Play? What would be an ideal RP?

I feel like I role play all the time. I always use a British accent, lol…I'd be a Queen, they'd be my peasant and have to do whatever I want.

Favorite position(s) and why?

Doggy style is the 1st that comes to mind, 69, and Missionary for the deep intimacy. Doggy style is the best way to reach my G-Spot

What is so special about sexual intercourse with you?

It's an experience. It's a spiritual one and you will feel it. Not everyone gets access to me. Many people are scared of that spiritual depth. Pussy is power

Masturbation: How often, what do you do/use?

I use either my hands or Rose-toy, sometimes even the showerhead. I just touch on myself until I come. At least 2x a week usually.

What do you desire to be done to you?

To be with someone who will have their way with me and take me to another dimension, and I also love to have my throat grabbed.

What's the wildest thing you've ever done or were asked to do sexually?

28

Richard "Shake" White

I don't feel as though I have done anything wild. But the wildest thing I've been asked to let a group of people have their way with me.

What are your thoughts on 3-somes/orgies?

I'm not opposed to those, those are fine, just no more than 4 people, I actually love 3-somes. I've only had a 3-some once though.

Have you ever participated in a 3-some/orgy? How was it? Would you do it again?

Yes. I absolutely see that in my near future, it's coming, literally and figuratively

What could be improved about your 3-some/orgy experience?

The partners. Also being more stimulating and intimate. It was just "Oh we're having a 3-some, let's get into it."

What do you think about casual sex between acquaintances/friends?

That one is real tricky. With certain boundaries in place it may work. We're adults. But at the same time… I don't know. It has to be a deeper connection, I'm not a casual person. But if you have those boundaries, I guess it's ok

What signs do you give off to let someone know that 'they can get it'?

That's questionable. I have to be physical with you, like me making the first move or allowing you to touch me. That's how you would know. Like an intimate type of touching. I'm very vocal, so I'll let you know. So there's no guesswork.

How would you like to be asked/propositioned for a sexual encounter?

I like to be intrigued; I like to see what people have to say. I'm very open-minded, apply that pressure. I like to see if they're all talk or whatever. Stimulate my mind. I like to see how people move.

How much does size matter to you? (Total Body ie stomach, breast, booty, lips, penis, clit etc.)

Size has never mattered to me; I've dated all sizes with both men and women. Size isn't important, I'm more concerned about how someone treats me. I don't think I have a type.

Bonus: What is your advice that wasn't covered in the questions asked?

Knowing your partner on a spiritual level plays a big part of love making and sex. Coming at them about sex all the time when they have so much negativity going on in life isn't good. Energy transfers.

Richard "Shake" White

HARD!

Richard "Shake" White

Big Girls

Relax and enjoy my touch
Legs hoisted up
Moist enough to drown on the way down
Face down, mid-day, I'm enjoying lunch
Got you in my clutch and grasp
With all that ass, you didn't expect me to pick you up
Dick you down and lick you up
Flipping you around to lick your butt
Spreading your cheeks
I love to eat as much as you do
And I will prove to you
My reach is deep enough to go through you
Hit your spots
You on top when you want to be
Tabletop with you in front of me
Or legs wrapped around when you're under me
Sucking your double-D's
Hugging me lovingly
Me stuffing your muffin, we cumming together
Kiss you from head to heel
I want you to feel me in your torso
Doggy style, keep you filled with this Cane Corso
Command and I'll obey, I know how to treat it
Don't be afraid to sit on my face,
Forget about weight as I eat it...
Baby, I'll make you feel like the only thing heavy about you is the breathing
You've got beauty, curves, tits, hips, thighs, plus size
A plush side and desire to ride
And I'd be honored to oblige
Let each ounce, pound, and inch be appreciated like they're supposed to
Grab you every time I approach you
Cause I've got to have it whenever I'm close to
"Sweet Nothings," I can't tell you as well as I can show you
I know you...
Self-conscious about your figure

35

But my appetite bigger
I may be slimmer than you like, but I fit perfectly
Parallel, horizontally, or vertically
And when you hunger and thirst for me
Certainly, I'll rise to the occasion like heat and mercury
Explore your Venus, tongue probing your anus (Uranus), diving into your depths
Everything should be wet...
I like when all the cushion pushing I'm doing
Got us moving across the room
Don't cover your stomach when I'm looking
I'm appreciating the view
I'm appreciating the you you gave; no shame
When you came, I bathed in your waves
Grave digger, I tunnel deep for the body
If ever you crave for any part of me, it's a party
I'll bring the favors, you bring the flavors
And we can savor one another
Those breasts, thighs, and yams should be smothered in euphoria
Looking forward to more of you
Kissing, licking, rubbing, and touching you
You know as well as I do that big girls need Fucking Too.

Richard "Shake" White

We Should

I should lick and kiss in between your hips
Then you should lick the you off these lips
The dew, the midst
We shouldn't miss a moment, a movement
You want it, we should do it
I should be fluent in your fluids before we finish
Fuck my face
Handcuffed, don't try to escape
We should create a safe word,
And fuck through it
I should grab you, gag you
Prop your ass up on the sink in the bathroom
And have you -begging me to forgive you for doubting me
You should have your mouth on me,
Your ass should bounce on me while gripping me
You should just strip for me
Let your lips massage the tip for me
Let it slip for me
You should let me enter and exchange energies
We should make memories, music and messes
Our sexing should make us forget all about our exes
You should come back for seconds
And we should enjoy every minute from start to finish
We should have witnesses watching through windows wondering why
we aren't worn out
Truthfully, we should be worn out...
You should name the time and place
You should climb my face, grind my face
I should be so deep in you I can't find my waist
We should be so familiar that I can describe how you climaxing tastes
We should learn from mistakes and practice perfecting
We should get naked, no secrets to hide
Turn on your side, use my hands and guide me
Hit that stride
I should know how you feel inside when I fill your insides
Levees breached til we wet the sheets
You should feel my heartbeat against your walls when nature calls

37

You should answer, you should be my private dancer, and I your musician

We should be a painted picture, perfectly placed in our favorite position

We should get it, you should admit it

You want it as much as I do

Let me lay beside you, finger tracing that side view before diving inside you

Undressing your stress

I want your soul, body and mind nude

We should take our time with every meeting

Every scar, stretch mark, and freckle deserves a proper greeting

You shouldn't rush me when I'm eating

I should be pleasing you as I'm pleased with you

I should be on my knees with you, both going down with the ship

You should take pride in this dick, instead of just riding this dick

My lips colliding with clit

Your lips should engulf me, I should be "killing it softly" often enough to never be misunderstood

We could make being this bad feel so good...

We should

Richard "Shake" White

Misses Good-Good

She be so wet, you might slip
Be she be vice-like, tight grip
Bites lip
Then she takes it all, she don't just ride tip
She likes to reverse-cowgirl so you can watch as she sits back and hides dick
Her thighs thick
Hips, ass as perfectly shaped
As the way she tastes
She makes, her cat purr-fect
Takes me in the back of her - neck
She's got that warm mouth
She's got that, make you pull up, but can't seem to pull out
She's got that, "Wait a minute"
Maybe make you put a baby in it if you ain't strapped with wrapping
Within those walls, her halls filled with liquid satin
Silk, her milk and honey yummy
She holds my face in it when I'm tasting it
Makes sure I ain't wasting a drop
She says, "Go slower, get to know her"
Educated when she's giving me top
She gets that grip on it, puts lips on it
The way she licks on it and spits on it
Her head game is bob and weave
Throat hits, stick and move when she jabs
Speed bag, heave, gag
Depth control, she's got breath control
When she goes down she can go rounds
Mouthpiece
She likes to perform...
Watch porn and weather the storm
Avalanche, she comes down right on top of me
Rocking me
Mopping me with she, she don't be stopping
Hopping, dropping and popping
Tearing through fishnet stockings...

She likes her toes sucked, throat clenched, and her hair pulled
Ass grabbed, both hands full
When it comes to me, she's an addict
Whenever I cum she likes to take time and meditate, roll one and medicate
And then gets right back at it
Lips to tip like she's puff, puff, passing
She's got a habit of having the most passionate actions that I can imagine
It's like she ain't done until I'm gasping and flaccid
Though she be running when she's coming, she be coming back
When I cum she wants it on her stomach, back
Running down her crack and lap
She does everything right, the way I like
She's so exact
We act... Like Honey Badger meets Tasmanian Devil
Our love making is on another level
Creating music, bass, treble
As I strum her strings and she plays my wood
Her name...
Is Misses Good-Good

Richard "Shake" White

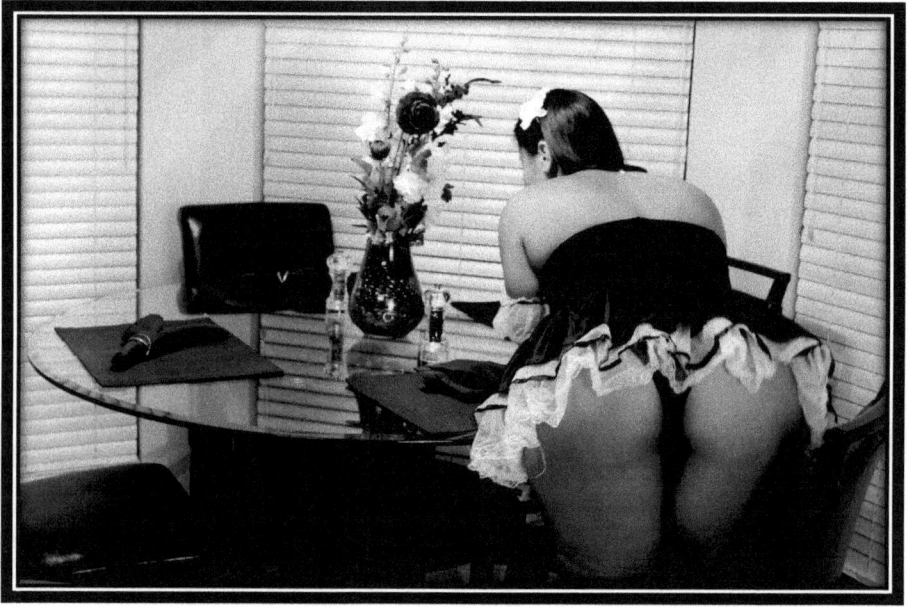

Richard "Shake" White

Breakfast in Bed

I woke up in her mouth...
Eyes wide opened
Fully throated, she's stroking her lotus
I can see the focus on her face, I must taste like hopes and dreams
The way she gripped, slurped and slobbed,
Gagged with every bob
The way she creams and cums as soon as her petals are touching my
tongue
Sensually, gently, and vigorous, tongue stroking her clitoris
This is our body-language's way of thanking us for being intimate
We're just restarting what we've finished
Smells the "Last Night" in the sheets
When we were just two insomniacs rocking each other to sleep
Had the room's temperature running on fever
I couldn't have gone any deeper
And when she went down on me, my lips went down to meet her,
greet her
I didn't stop at filling the void, I gave like I was meant to complete her
Treated her to Heaven on Earth the way my girth parted her seas ...
I'm guided in with ease
Both hands gripping the undersides of her knees
Making sure the 'Wild' inside of her was seized
Our eyes locked,
She bit her lip, gripped tighter
Whether throwing it back or running away
She kept me deep inside her
She provided the goods
Keeping the fire burning inside of us
I was providing the wood
Then back to my tongue reminding her hood
to come off the head...
The way she was gripping the mattress, causing the sheets to come off
of the bed
Even when her mouth is full, I know how to listen
She was done being submissive, wanting to switch positions
Back on my back, I laid
She sat, and came, her walls caved
I started smacking her ass for how badly she misbehaved

43

She gave ovations while she twerked on it
She put a hurt on it, then played nurse on it
Money shot, she bet the purse on it,
Then slurped on it
She began and ended with head; we both were fed...
Breakfast in bed

Richard "Shake" White

What I realized while missing you...
Is that I'm in love with the thick of you
Sticking this dick in you
Kissing you
I don't need to mention you to picture you
Forgetting you isn't permissible
I've done things to you in my dreams that I should've asked permission
to
I don't need an interview to raise and center you
My mission to position you in ways to enter you
Giving you reasons to stay and misbehave
Giving praise while I play and lay in your waves
Straight A's when I grade
Maydays when I cockpit, I'm going down
Shower me with love, I wanna drown
I feel like that's my honey and I want it now...
What I've realized...
Is how crazy it sounds to be addicted to dicking you before ever
putting some dick in you
I'm so in to you I'm sick of you
Maybe that's just withdrawals and starvation
That causes this heart's racing
An inpatient of impatience
Wanting your therapy on the couch to talk to it
Show you I can both, appreciate and berate it
I'm not afraid to be rated,
I guarantee to eat it better than he ate it
He ain't it
I promise not a moment nor drop would be wasted
If you let me taste it, by now we should be naked
What I've realized...
I can't control these cravings for consumption
When you want something, like I want something
Nothing else will do but you
I'm talking breakfast, brunch, and luncheon
Get it in again for dinner and dessert
And if it hurts, I'll nurse it back perfectly

Keep serving me emission-causing visions
Of you sucking me into submission
Head-on collisions, wet conditions
Let me learn the landscape
I'll listen to your body and translate
Until you can't stand straight, walk funny
I mentally orgasm every time you talk to me
Raw honey, it be(e) like that
Just know when your flower drains all my power
I'll be right back
I'm sure I've got to do more than beat it up
The way she fight back
I've seen this scene in a dream
Where your 2 (tulips) lips rose to my fly, trapped me inside
And once you had me inside, you were happy inside
From the back, from the side, you were even happy to ride
Wet walls were so warm I felt I had to reside
What I've realized...
Is that you must feel like home the way you make this man cave
Fighting so hard to behave, stave, stray and stay away
Yet no matter what I cut; I just want to stage the play
Supporting cast, my hands... support your ass
As our pelvics clash and thrust
I know... without you, there can be no Us
I keep telling me "Don't lust."
But as much as I want your touch
To taste, see, smell, and hear you it's senseless
So since it's... Such a sensitive subject to stomach
I'll sit silently, secretly seeking some sort of sign
That screams, "It's time to treat your body like it's mine"
And in the meantime, keep it disguised
I've realized...
That I can't get you out of mind

Richard "Shake" White

She Can't

She can't refuse it…
Got her stuck on this new dick, like a glue stick
I be trying to abuse it… when we do it
She said I should cum "tool bags and business cards" cause I definitely
know what I'm doing
I've got that work
I got that make you squirt before you get out of that skirt
That you want me to beat it, but I got to eat it up first
That, do I need to gag you with my shirt, you're screaming "Wait big
daddy it hurt" or "Oh my gawd your girth"
She can't get enough…
She likes it rough and deep, wants to be rocked to sleep
I make that ass "drop" and "leap," she gotta hop to keep pace
She gonna leak and waste before I'm reaching 3rd base
Cum on my face when I taste before sliding into home plate
She's into fishnets and red bottoms, but I'm just trying to make that
bottom red,
She be giving bobble head, that "too good not to swallow head,"
better than every X-men
She give me that "Ms. Marvel" head/ legs spread, toes curled- she
bucking back, I'm thrusting… I'm getting stomach…I like to feel the
"breeze" when she blow, that crown and drown, those… burping and
slurping sounds is all I hear out there
She can't keep quiet…
It's like I penetrate the silence when I'm inside it
Its sounding like a riot, she releasing the hydrants and the sirens- make
that sound: J. Holiday… I eat that ass, brown and round, every day is
a holiday
Candles lit, perfect fit when she grips- love how she be biting her lip
when she riding the dick
She be trying to out- muscle this muscle and muzzle her mouth
But these walls can't muffle the sound- she's so loud it sounds like I'm
putting it down on a crowd
She can't handle this alone…
She be on the phone, calling other chicks to bone
Searching for another pair of thick hips to ride the throne

47

She knows she's on her own when we get home, so when we roam, she prefers I make another woman moan, she only stop watching to give me dome… she say "two heads are better than one," as long as she's the one that gets the cum
She don't mind a 3-some, I'm pleasing one with my tongue
My head got her head sprung- She trying to make king-dome-cum
She can't stand the rain…
She loves my deep strokes as much as I love her deep throat
But it's like she can't stand the pain, she gone swallow when it spit- so I don't have to aim
She's parasitic … I mean sucks like a leech, slurred speech
Even my balls feel the walls of her jaws and cheeks
My peak is steep, but she be taking it deep
She'd be on her knees if I weren't making them weak
We make fucking love, like we just love fucking
She says "Big daddy my cat "me oww"
But… she can't stop for nothing…
She wanna handle this dick like a champ…
But she can't

*Courtesy of previously published works written by Shake the poet (Richard White)

Richard "Shake" White

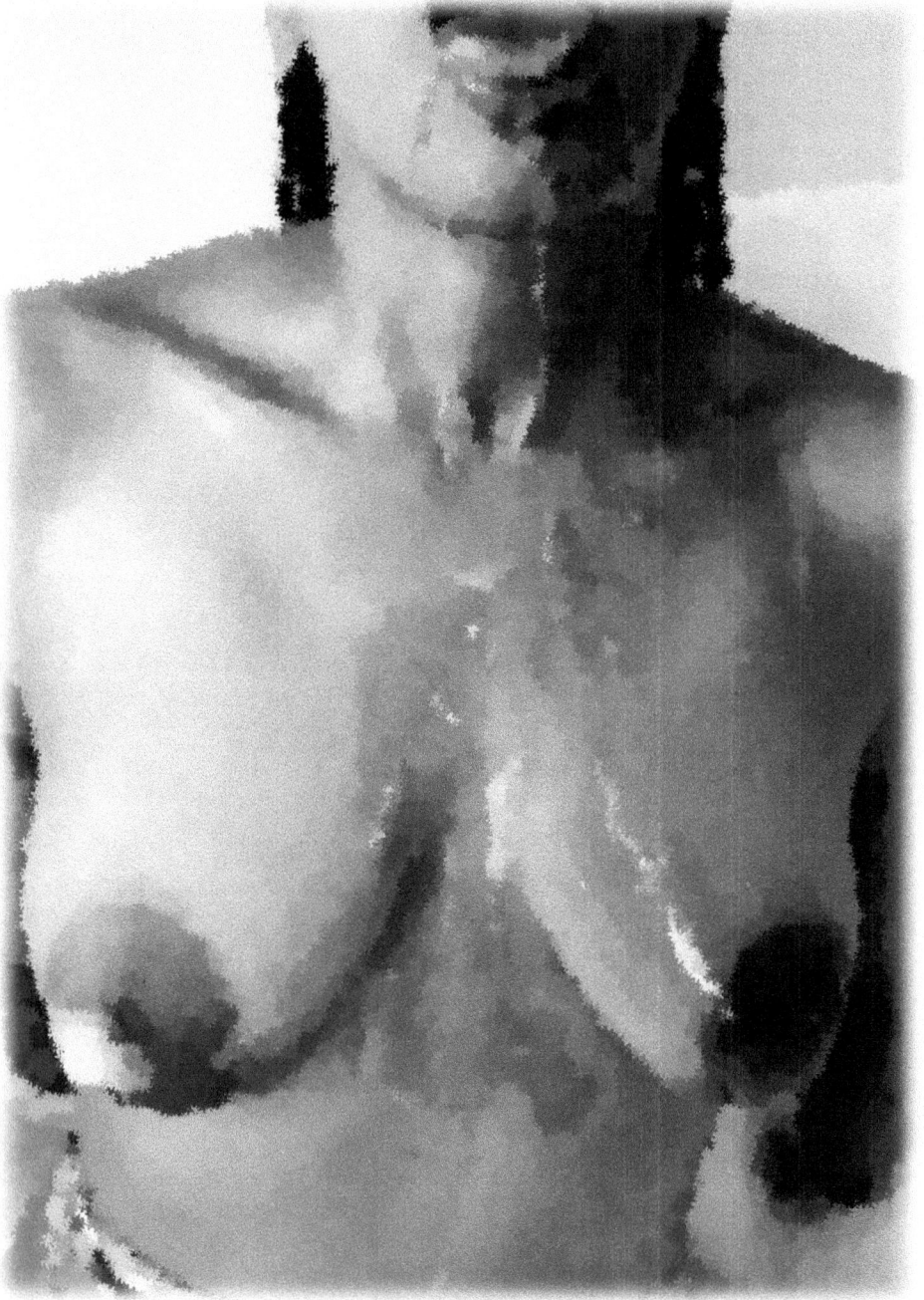

Richard "Shake" White

The Lickening

Every time I'm in your orbit my temperatures rise
Maybe it's just in my mind, but I can feel the intensity climb
So tonight, Let it be about performance and endurance
Don't you worry, I'll be changing the sheets in the morning
No more ignoring the signs
I'm trying to have your love pour over mine
Lick you from waist beads to toe-ring
Kiss you from neck to navel, taste you
Dive deep like you went overboard and it's my job to save you
Rescue, make you run up walls and fetch you, chase you
Get so nasty with your body that I should be ashamed to face you...
Every time you walk in the room, I start throbbing
Visions of your lips gripping and slobbering
With me slipping inside them
Kissing your flower
You having your poom-poom devoured
There's power in these lips, what I'm saying is...
I've got an oral fixation for tasting your most intimate places
Giving you face while creating sensations in spaces ranging from navel
to anal and all along your waist
Wasting not an inch of you, once my tongue enters you, you'll clench,
quiver, and shiver
Then I'll lick, slip, and slither, I come to deliver
Put my face in it, hands gripping your ass
Slurping and circling slow, yet flipping and flicking it fast
Gently pressing my lips against your labia
Acquainting with your clit
The more I indulge, the more you'll crave for this dick
And with every lick, lap, nibble and roll of my tongue
I'm anticipating the making and tasting you cum
Losing our senses... So sensitive
My lips glistening, I'm listening, hearing the sounds of sex
Even your silhouette is dripping wet
Performing pirouettes, pushing, pulling and pleasuring until I'm
pulsating
Tongue tracing those stretch marks on your tummy and pelvis
A glutton for your loving, render you helpless

51

Serviced, Selfless, but the way I'll eat it all
You'll swear that I'm selfish

Richard "Shake" White

Richard "Shake" White

**Manhandled**

One can imagine how you want to be tamed
From flicker to flame
Locking your wrists with these chains - cuffed
Those times when being touched ain't enough,
You want to be fucked and ravaged by a savage
Have your body sandwiched
A lot of ass smacking and titty grabbing
Having your love handles gripped
Inner thighs kissed, clitoris licked
While your lips engulf a dick
1 hand clenching your neck, another locked in your locks
Both guiding you to and fro as you perform top on the cock
Or... Having your meatus and anus eaten simultaneous
We know...
You want us to go to war
To feel which one is wanting you more
Be the object of our desires
And when you tire... You don't want a break
You want to be broken
You want us to fill in every place that you can open
You want to be holding one, with the other holding you
So, you can't run from me
You were lonely and Three's Company
We're all in agreement
Sometimes you want both the Beasts & Behemoths
Be that rare meat between us, and feed us
You get a rise from pain
You want to ride this train
Neither he nor I mind, we admire that you don't hide in shame
You're more than 1 man can handle, you say
Touché
We came ready to accommodate the way that you play, do whatever
you say
We heard you...
No misinterpretations, we're certain you want the stimulations, and
penetrations that leads to asphyxiation and perspiration
You don't just want to fuck, you want to get stuck

55

Between a rock and a hard place
Make your thighs part ways
Face buried in your front, your back
Two hands gripping your rack,
Two hands caressing your back
Saliva sliding down from your crack
His head in your ass, My head in your lap
If you like it like that
Licking the libations left on your legs, awaiting further commands
We understand
That sometimes
You want to be handled...
By more than 1 man.

Richard "Shake" White

Three

I dreamt…
you were in my bed, legs spread, and I can't get that head out of my head – face time
She was faced down, drowning in you
mouth covered in dew, in you and you…
caressed your breasts as I watched - voyeurism
I enjoyed the vision as y'all switched positions, bodies kissing
Hissing and slurping sounds mixed with moans made music, moved me – closer
My face in you, your face in She and we… ate like kings, royalty
My loyalty to her and lust for you, as you two became more acquainted
Painted love notes that spoke in body language
No explanation necessary, sexy – very
Derrieres in the air, pear-shaped, apple-bottom
Me… drunk off the juice from your fruits
It was as if, this was the first time your body was truly touched, had your fupa sucked
Love handles grabbed with passion, abdomen spasms, as I'm smashing your back in
Thumb in your crack, your lips smacking in her passionfruit
While you're eating her rose, I'm sucking her toes – slow, with every stroke
Grabbing you by the throat, you choking She
She loving every stroke of your tongue, She cums, then you do
Pulsating as I moved through you, She - pulling closer to you
Longing to see how this tantra suits you, Kama Sutra
Her legs braid with yours like two sensual, scissors insisting on entering each other's incisions
As they glisten, I'm watching your bodies rocking by candle flame
My inner animal came to handle and tame
to dismantle your frames from passion, minus the pain
She mounts… slips down my tip, you sit on these lips
My tongue, parting your labia, tasting you, you wasting upon my face
Both of y'all's hips race faster than hearts beating
Me eating - you kissing - she - riding me and we…

Came 3 times each at least, before She just wanted to watch you with me

Me – still throbbing, you engulfing, slobbing, bobbing - tongue running up and down my shaft

She cums – from touching herself to spreading your ass

Her tongue runs up and down your crack and back, and back

Until you sat on my lap, legs wrapped, strapped 'round my waist

Face to face, and I could taste 'Us' on your lips

She… licking your hips, kissing your dips, and biting your lips

Taking control like She's writing the script

She sips some wine, then sits on mine

As our lips meet and speak, she sucks your peaks, nibbles your nipples

Grabs your ass, as to ask you to move faster and after you've creamed and came

She came to clean you

Strumming your vulva, your meatus, taking you places penetration passes by and I…

I bury my face in her… and She purrs

She whispers… that, "Two heads are better than one, and this one… She prefers"

I dreamt… and I ain't been awake since

*Courtesy of previously published works written by Shake the poet (Richard White)

Richard "Shake" White

Richard "Shake" White

Sometimes you've got to break the rules
And play with your food
That 2-finger flick, while my lips grip the clit...
I've got to whisper and hum to it
So gentle you cum to it
That cat calls, I run to it
I know when to get rough, grip and touch
When you want me to run through it
That Cat & Mouse chase...
I only come up for air when you ask, "How that mouth taste"
Back to those slow, sensual circles, the sucking, slobbering, and slurping
Patient, I'm waiting for the "Throwing it back" and twerking
I like, how you like, that I always know how to work it
Your orgasms are my purpose, my pleasure
I've got to dig for the treasure
Hit a geyser, a gusher
When I touch cha'
I want it to feel so good you start to suffer,
Pitfalls...
Withdrawals...
Deep when I breach, my reach hits walls
Balls slap against crack, our laps smacking, your ass clapping
A lot of climaxing is happening
Dampening the mattress, the sheets
Until the duvet covers are smothered in our cum and loving
I'll keep you coming back... for more
And when my back is sore, you come and ride it
and when you're too tired to climb it
I'll get behind it, slip inside it, massaging yours at the same time
Learning all your secrets like I heard them through the grapevine
At any time, peeling through your Apple-bottoms, eating your peach until I make wine
Taste divine, I hate to be wasting time
So when I smack that ass, I smack that ass like it's payback for having to wait in line
We should've been crossed this bridge

Pressing your ribs against the fridge,
Your face against the ice box
Claiming my territory, renaming it "My Spot"
It gets hot in the kitchen
Wet like the sprinklers dripping, there's finger licking
Spreading you across the counter, then burying my face inside your flower
Covering your mouth, cause any louder you'd be disturbing our neighbors
Love (Fuck) you in the shower about an hour later
Savoring every moment...
Promise I'll talk to it like I own it
Deep conversations and body language
Listening to the way every moan tries to explain it
Reminding me of what I'm supposed to do
Like she - begging me - to go back to choking and stroking you
I've got ahold of you, but you the one ain't letting go
I start sucking your toes, and touching erogenous zones
These thick lips kiss against your collar bone
Pussy so good it's falling off it,
I'm into your deep, dark, chocolate
Teach you what heaven feels like, I'll be your Prophet
Naked and nude, no better outfit
Tossing your salad, expanding my palate
I'm up for that challenge
You swore you were ready for
Have your legs like spaghetti, you're breathing heavy
Creaming every... wearing you out
Cum till we drought, fucking your mouth
You're my favorite flavor
Promise to keep the cunnilingus to fellatio ratio forever in your favor
Your body beckons...
In a minute, we'll have been at it for hours, and I'm already wanting seconds

Richard "Shake" White

Unavailable

I understand, let's talk about your man
The plan
Is to keep your head so high in the clouds I can hold deep
conversations with your kitty
"Does he love you enough to learn the language? Come here, Dame
un Beso"
You are, only spoken for if you say so…
So before you say, "No" and begin talking about what he would do
Let's discuss what pleases you and just ease into me eating you
I know that's blunt, but your walls are up
This is just me breaching you
Learning you, I'm eager to
A hard study, digging up a degree in you
A PHd that won't throw off your PH-B
Balancing his "Baby I promise you"'s with daily déjà vu's of our
rendezvous, if you allow me to
I want to drown in you
Hear the sounds you make, get you naked
And bathe in compliments any parts you hate
Stretch marks, moles, or scar tissue
Every part of you, create a spark with you
So in tune with your body, you won't know when it's you or the kitty
that I'm talking to
You're feeling drained, I know what to pour in you
Through these lips, my tongue runs laps, takes tours of you
I'm sure you're a freak in the sheets, let me release the whore in ya
Our secret
Save me in your phone as Victoria
Or Dr. Downs, Dick U.
Your OB-Gyn, Mr. All the way in
A necessary sin, a guilty pleasure
I will be your new Ruler where he can't measure up
We can make love or fuck
You can hit the blunt while I'm eating it up
Deep in your guts or dick in your Butt
Hell, he can cuck if you want, if he can handle it

63

I'm here to keep your candle lit, when he can't manage it
The sweet and sensual or that savage shit
So whenever you want me to unwrap the package and ravage it
Have you orgasming back to back to back like bad habit shit
You can have it
A master of mattress magic,
Maestro of making music of your moans
Leaving you pleasantly pulsating like the lips of your pussy was spitting
poems, I'm just saying
Cause your legs to shake like that's what they call me
So call me, I'll be waiting
Turn your masturbation to penetration, more pure sensations
Touch your yoni, your body pours libations
Our body language conversation be deeper than politics and religion
With me it's a give in, you'll always be sitting in a different position,
getting different positions
Let me fill the prescription
That leaves you smitten and dripping long after
Side Effects are stress forgetting, so that stress you're getting won't
matter
But rather, when and where we'll gather
Just make time, I'll make time, I won't waste time
I'll devour, I won't just taste, dine
Your body, I'll strafe, climb
Claim and make mine
Pleasure and pamper, then occasionally beat it like a hate crime
This ain't smoke and mirrors I'm selling you
I'm just telling you
So tell me
When do you think you'll become available

Richard "Shake" White

The Interviews (3)

Describe your sexual preference/orientation (ex. Bi, Poly, etc)
I guess currently it would be Bi
Do you prefer sensuality over physicality? (love making or fucking) explain?
Sensuality. It's more personal. I'm real sensitive to touch.
What is the easiest way to turn you on / what turns you off?
I'm really turned on by smart mother fuckers. I like to kiss, that's 1 of my biggest things. Since I'm sensitive to touch, almost anywhere you kiss and touch me is a big turn on. Also, I don't like really strong scents, but when you smell good that's a really good thing too. Super sloppy kisses are a turn off.
Describe an ideal sexual encounter with you?
I like romantic shit… like a surprise trip like on a beach or a balcony and it's sensual and intimate
How do you perform cunnilingus/fellatio? (give tips and tricks?)
I like to be thorough… play with the balls, make sure I get it wet enough. Both hands or no hands whichever they prefer, and sucking on the balls.
How do you like oral to be performed on you? (give tips and tricks)
It's more so what I don't like. I just need clitoral stimulation… I don't want to be fingered or a lot of spit.
How do you feel about anal? (oral, penetration, toys etc)
That it is absolutely fabulous. I love it. it took a while for me to get the penetration, but once you relax…. I love it
How do you feel about bondage? (ever tried it)
I don't like that. I don't like not being in control
What are your thoughts on Role Play? What would be an ideal RP?
RP sounds fun, I haven't done it. What I would like is to pretend we don't know each other at a Bar and go at it. I feel like that would give the "1 night-stand" kinda element
Favorite position(s) and why?

From the back, because they can go all in and I like my ass being smacked. The other one... maybe being on top, but it depends on the dick

What is so special about sexual intercourse with you?

Like I said before, I'm very thorough. Whatever I like to do, I like to do it well. I won't stop until it's done right. Like giving you head, I won't stop until you're finished. Whatever needs to happen, I'll make it happen

Masturbation: How often, what do you do/use?

Pretty often, between 4/5 per week. I use a massage gun now because it's real strong, or the shower head. That's been the go-to for years. I don't like using my hands because it takes too long.

What do you desire to be done to you?

A lot of things, I like to be choked, slapping is cool, but not too hard. I like my toes being sucked...that's a big thing. Finger or 2 in my ass or tongue, head of course

What's the wildest thing you ever done or were asked to do sexually?

This 1 guy wanted me to finger his ass. We didn't do anything else, he just wanted me to play with his ass

What are your thoughts on 3-somes/orgies?

I've had them before, they can be overrated. I think I'd prefer MFM, make it more about the female

Have you ever participated in a 3-some/orgy? How was it? Would you do it again?

Yes, it was alright, but I get bored with the other female

What could be improved about your 3-some/orgy experience?

More dicks, lol...MFM instead of FMF

What do you think about casual sex between acquaintances/friends?

It could get messy. I've had that situation before and the guy ended up wanting to be with me. Probably not a good idea cause people tend to catch feelings

What signs do you give off to let someone know that 'they can get it'?

66

There's a certain way that I look at them. If they're not getting it, then maybe a little brush of the leg, a little sensual touch. If all else fails then just jump on the dick

How would you like to be asked/propositioned for a sexual encounter?

If I know the person, they'd have to be subtle and smooth with it, they can't be like "lets fuck". If I don't know them, they've got to woo me, make it worth my while. Why should I fuck you, state your case

How much does size matter to you? (Total Body ie stomach, breast, booty, lips, penis, clit etc)

Titties, I like …at least a B or C cup. I like ass, something I can grab onto. You gotta have some dick. I prefer a curve.

Bonus: What is your advice that wasn't covered in the questions asked?

Be more involved and be willing to do whatever. Listening to want I want is important, pay attention to ME, don't just do what feels good to you.

The Interviews (4)

Describe your sexual preference/orientation (ex. Bi, Poly, etc)
Heterosexual, I prefer bio males

Do you prefer sensuality over physicality? (love making or fucking) explain?

Depends on the individual. Some people as soon as you see them it's sexual, you just want to know what that thing about. Then there are others who may change your mind and become sensual, then others you know off the bat that it's about love making.

What is the easiest way to turn you on / what turns you off?

Not into super aggressive men. You can be confident, and cocky but not aggressive. Someone can lose my respect and interest by saying the wrong thing. I don't like a person who is not authentic. I don't like men who lead with their money, means or status, complete turn off. Financial irresponsibility. Don't take care of their kids.

Turn ons... Men who take the time to get to know me, without judgement. Men who say, "I want to get to know all of you, not just the pretty parts of you". Intelligent men, sense of humor, who doesn't take himself too seriously.

Describe an ideal sexual encounter with you

I prefer the unexpected... I'm definitely not vanilla. I might have been Sheila last time, today, I might be Nicole. I love spontaneity. I want all the attention on me, I wouldn't be a good 3-some partner.

How do you perform cunnilingus/fellatio? (give tips and tricks)

I won't say that I am a professional in that area. I would say that I'm a novice. I think we should ask our partner likes and give it to them. He may want you to lick the shaft, or just the head etc. You got to be open to learning. If your partner wants to try new things, you should be open to try.

How do you like oral to be performed on you? (give tips and tricks)

I will let a person try their technique, hoping they'll recognize what I don't like. I'll give them the signs. I get the most stimulation from oral. You gotta be multi-talented to deal with me. I'm not for the faint of heart, you're gonna put in some work.

How do you feel about anal? (oral, penetration, toys etc)

I don't have a problem with it. I've tried it. Size is a thing. It takes the body some time to COME BACK to where it needs to be. I don't mind beads etc. I would have to be comfortable with the person for that activity to even be on the board. But in that moment, with the right person...I don't think anything is off the board.

How do you feel about bondage? (ever tried it)

I think I would be into it. I've tried it light, but not much. It is intriguing to me... I'm in control of my life and in that action, I don't have any control. I've never been pushed past my limit,

68

and when bound, I have no control of that. I can't say if that's a good or bad thing cause I haven't been there

What are your thoughts on Role Play? What would be an ideal RP?

Can be a good thing, it's a spice thing. After a while sex becomes monotonous, no matter how freaky you are. It keeps you spicy, keeps you intrigued. In relationships sex becomes routine, so this helps bring excitement to the activity.

Favorite position(s) and why?

From the back. In my opinion, visually for ya'll that's the sexiest thing for yall. It makes it look like yall are dominating us, and the energy that a man gives when hitting it from the back, is just different. It's the most primal, animalistic sexual encounter. No one gives a damn if you're comfortable, let's get it. I also, like positions where I am positioned above the man so I can look down on him. I hate missionary. I have long legs so riding tends to be uncomfortable when done for long periods.

What is so special about sexual intercourse with you?

Honestly and truthfully, the fact that I do it. I'm single, live by myself, so if I'm having sex with you and potentially wasting my time, you should be honored. I've had terrible sex for years.

Masturbation: How often, what do you do/use?

Not often. Masturbation doesn't make sense to me because I'm a sensual person. I don't want to be by myself, I want to be hugged, see sweat glistening and know that I just put in some work. I would much rather a person in me than an apparatus

What do you desire to be done to you?

I think it would go back to bondage. I would like to meet a man that I'm so comfortable with, that I wouldn't say No to him. I enjoy men who can't get theirs if I don't get mine. Talk crazy to me

What are your thoughts on 3-somes/orgies?

I don't mind them if that's your thing. I would like to go to a swinger party and observe, then my partner and I go home. I could see myself doing voyeurism or being an exhibitionist tho

What do you think about casual sex between acquaintances/friends?

In theory it makes sense but in reality, it doesn't. I haven't seen it work out well. If you and your friend are having sex, then you're into each other. You have to be willing to take the risk of potentially losing that friend.

What signs do you give off to let someone know that 'they can get it'?

I'm very straight forward. If I'm not telling you that I want it, then I probably don't. If I want it, you'll know cause we're gonna do it. I'll just start taking your clothes off. Just depends on my comfort level with the person.

How would you like to be asked/propositioned for a sexual encounter?

I don't like to be asked. You got to read the moment. When a woman wants to have sex with you, you'll know.

How much does size matter to you? (Total Body ie stomach, breast, booty, lips, penis, clit etc.)

I've had a little bit of everything, that being said…my preference is a normal body type. I've learned that slender fellas tend to have more of a package…. soooo based on my observations, lol. Overweight… you better have a great personality and some change in your pocket from time to time…I expect the sex to be wack

Richard "Shake" White

Richard "Shake" White

!HARDER!

Richard "Shake" White

Place it on my face, let me taste it until I can figure out the recipe...
I want to behave recklessly
Hennessey and ecstasy
Eat it until nothing's left, yet we...
Just getting started...
Caramel and Chocolate
Kundalini and Cunnilingus keeping you cumming
Conscious wavering, I'm savoring you on my lips and goatee
Anticipating for your grip to hold me
Entering slowly
Our connection feeling familiar
Yet your Flower is just getting to know me
You're running from the strumming of my tongue
G-spot, Deep Spots, Clitoris, Vaginal Walls, and Vulva
Then turning you over to tantalize
Tongue tickling, touching, and twisting, have you twitching
Lips smack, lick up your crack to the small of your back
Stay in this position...
Let me take a minute and touch you
Finger paint massage oils and hot wax into your tired muscles
Heels, calves, - thighs, ass, - back, shoulders, neck
In my clutch our touch is not to be broken
This is to tease and tenderize before I go in
Fingertips deep in your scalp massaging along your sew-in
Burying your face in, the way I had previously buried mine
Fingers glide sensually back down your spine
Grabbing my pride, sliding it inside from behind
No, I don't mind if you whine and beg
But I'm pulling out to be sure you're fed
Maybe give you more head instead if I feel so inclined
6's and 9's
I'm putting time in before I get mine in
Aligning your spine and chakras, your soul is mine
Seeking to find how many more ways to make you feel even more
alive
Wrap me in your thighs, contact with the eyes
Kissing, sucking, nibbling on your breasts

Then gripping on your neck
Slightly stripping you of breath
You grip tighter my erect
Pull me closer like 'protect'
Our hearts beat symphonies into our chests
A mess will be made...
And we can hear the thickness of the moisture
Hoist your hips for even deeper dips
Catch a glimpse of the way its lips grip
Such a slick, slippery, sticky, and silky dick (Rich)
All over our skin wet, spit, sweat
Anticipating the position changes we haven't did yet
Feel me up in your ribs, chest
Turning you sideways, your right leg onto my shoulder
Continuing to stroke ya, holding my composure
Don't want to explode before the Wheelbarrow and Mower
I've got more to show ya, teach ya
I can get deeper, Baby you ain't got a secret that I'm unable to reach
Turning your navel towards the sheets, I'll keep your legs suspended
So hard up in it, so far up in it
Reaching for your heart like I can feel and heal the scars up in it
This ain't your first time, so I'm trying to raise the bar up in it
So good to your body it's like I'm trying to get right with God, find
forgiveness for my faults up in it
This is an informal apology for all the Ex's you've had sex with
Whenever you felt neglected by whomever you shared a bed with
I pay close attention; your satisfaction is an investment
It is said, "The best is yet to come," but you've done that a few times
Hypnotize your mind, before I lose mine
This is mine, so there's no confusion
Why I'm doing, what I'm doing, the way I'm doing it
Pleasing you is my mission, my movement
It'd be rude if I didn't prove it
Know how to find it and not lose it
How to be rough and not abuse it or bruise it
Trying to fuck your mind when the memories are running through it
So that every time your hands are roaming free...
You can think of only me when you do it.

Richard "Shake" White

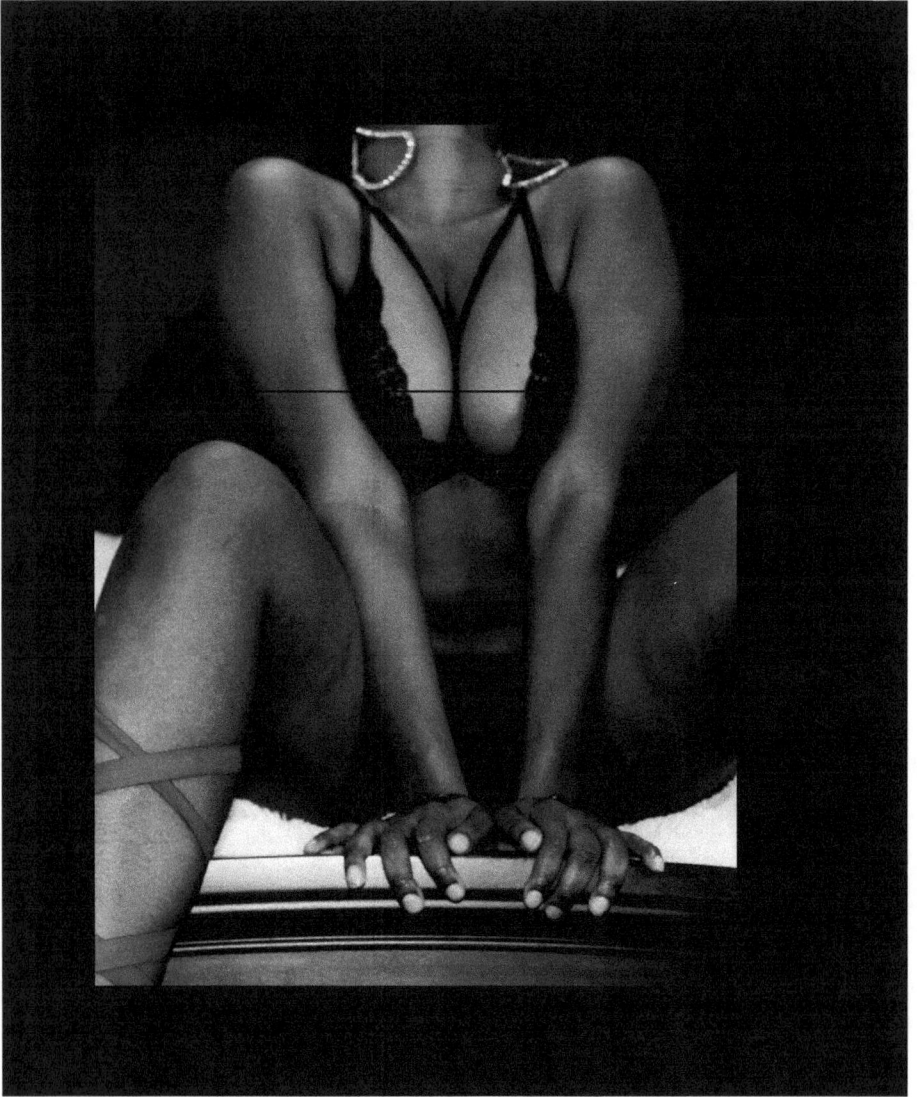

Richard "Shake" White

Educate me… teach me everything that you need
How you like to be squeezed, pleased, and relieved
And I will kiss, grip, and lick in script, perfect penmanship
Your clit, your slits, those nips, your lips, hips, your arches and dips
So when you arch it and dip
I can get deep enough to perform your autopsy, sloppy
Give you the god in me
Dichotomy, study your anatomy, then fuck you like you're mad at me
Navigate your biology until we both can see the astrology
I'm always ready to learn…
How to stimulate your G-spot - for so long that time stops, even though we not
We've got subject matter to discuss
I'm speaking directly through your skin, let me in
Learn me something…
To never be too slow, too fast, I won't fast at either eating coochie or ass
Take me to class, I'll pass with flying colors
Prying covers and sheets from your teeth
That therapy of speech kind of deep
That can't compete with how clearly you speak as we lay naked while I kiss massaging your feet
I listen, attention is paid, till all your tension is slain, paved against your inner walls
I lick them all
I can go down or sit you on top where you belong
So when we crown, it won't be just the head…
Every urge will be fed, every page will be read
Until I become familiar with your energy…
Until I learn to make your heart beat my name into your memory
I'm not the most prudent of students, never be rude in class
Raising my hands to learn any body language you utter, that causes a stutter
(My finger P-P-princess)
Stringing and strumming moans of different pitches and tones
Until you're left thinking that,
"Even when he's gone, wherever I roam, there's no place like home"

I jones to make honors, role play if you'd like
Picture perfect poetry poured upon your pussy, teach me how to write
How to ignite chakras, how to align yours with mine
Reciprocate, go in my bag, teach you the art of the 9-grabs
I'll find more ways to foreplay, I'm always in the lab
Teach me what I don't know
I'm pretty clever but getting better has never been a problem
Though I could find it blinded, knowing "How to" is the better option
I will… adapt, improvise and overcome, making you cum every time
you come over
With something new to expose to ya
Be glad you chose to get it like you're supposed to, any way you want
to
From leaving palm prints on the windows to having you faced down
fucking your eyeliner off into the pillows
Teach me… how to till your soil, flower your garden
How to get it right the first time, every time so there's never a need to
beg your pardon
A willing and eager participant ready to receive your masterclass
Learn how to grab your ass, how to punish it and doctor it
Earning my doctorate, my masters, multiple degrees in passion, I'm
asking…
For the lessons, the secrets, the keys to your secretions,
The needs that keep your inner demons fiending
Allow me – to be a student… of your teachings

Richard "Shake" White

___Sapiosexual___

Let's talk about it...
You may need an immense amount of dopamine to cope with me
I mean high enough to climb the walls and float with me
Fill your throat with me, gulping me as I open she
Performing perfectly like I've wrote the scene
So in tune with your body's language I can quote her,
I know her every note, and she is never off-key
Locksmith, so I'll turn her on, and never off me
There's a lot to be learned, let me enjoy teaching ya
Shutting down every form of media
So I can begin licking and flipping through the pages of your
encyclopedia,
Getting too know you
I'm sure to be greedier than whoever been eating ya
Maybe meatier for your needier side
Meeting your freakier side
And if you catch the fever to ride
I'll... have you gripping and dripping, while I'm slipping deeper
Pinning you down while I'm underneath her
And when you realize you need a breather...
You can just ride these soup coolers until I move you for new
maneuvers...
Let's talk about it
Lay our bodies perpendicular
So I can send shockwaves through your amygdala,
Don't be afraid...
The plan is to be so deep enough inside you that I can tell your age
Stimulate your perineum as soon as you spread your legs
Indulge my appetite until you beg to be fed
And while in the bed...
We can lay and embrace sensually, as we discuss centuries of history's
mysteries, or just me listening to your "wish-to-be's" and "meant-to-
be's"
We'll tend to be tender when we tend to each other
We be friends and lovers
Always up for that ménage à trios
With you, your pussy, and Moi

81

Let's talk about it
All night...
You'll have a Shakespearean experience
Until, "But soft! what light through yonder window breaks"
And as the Sun engulfs the Moon
I will big spoon and resume
Kissing up and down your spine while stroking you from behind
Fingers massaging your scalp, tips probing your mind
Intellect for breakfast, how thoughtful
Giving me brain like you love the taste of last night on me
Imagine being completely satisfied, yet still so horny
"Good morning" is how I greet you
I beseech you
Once again atop these lips seat you, eat you
There's been so many different ways I seen you, and each view
Should begin or end with you sitting on my face
Why waste that...
I could probably spend enough time studying your biology to
understand our astrology
Your anatomy flatters me, so when you're catching me casually licking
these lips with you in view; total observation
Just know... That I'm ready to have that conversation
...Let's Talk About It

Richard "Shake" White

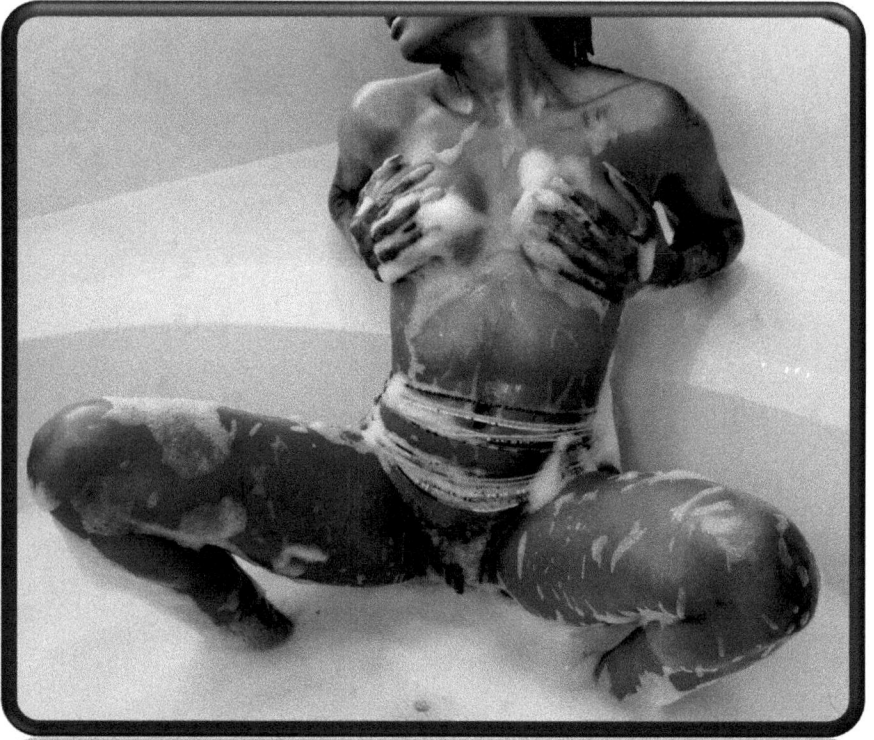

Richard "Shake" White

Dreamt of You

I've been asking if it's love
Afraid it might be
Envisions of you nightly
Right beside me
It's like we
Form storms, rain and lightning
Don't take this lightly
But I've wondered if in your dreams, do you seek to find me
I mean it's likely due to the fact that I think of you highly, mostly
Like with me is where you're supposed to be
Dreams of you standing so close to me
My chest against your back
Arms around your waist wrapped
Tapping into your senses, gripping
Kissing your neck, collarbone, earlobe, shoulder
Hands began caressing you all over
Breasts, stomach, slowly going lower
Your head turns to kiss, I begin sucking your lips
As my fingers slip from clit to slit until they drip of you
Last night I dreamt of you...
I see so vividly in my dreams, parts of you I've never seen
So I wonder...
If when my body screams for you, do you hear it's thunder
My eye's raindrops stop falling when they call for you
I see you there, bare, wearing nothing but me out
Now hear me out...
Spiritually, emotionally, I'm still learning, but I believe physically I've
got it figured out
And...
I bet it be so tight, you can't prick a thorn in it
I bet it give me life like I was born in it...
Like Autumns in New York, I can burrow deep and keep warm in it
Hung like an ornament, there's a storm pending
Feel the forming of flash flood warnings
Prefer the oral performance
But it feels safer inside...
What if I...

85

Slide down your legs, lick the bottom of your foot from heel to arch
Until I feel them part
Take a sip from your well to heal when feeling parched
Bathe and baptize my body in your beauty
While wandering where your wetness welcomes this work
It'd be my duty
My honor, and obligation
To allow for domination, but not until after my domination
I'm sure you can take it, get naked and let me make it mine
Claiming it, licking my name in it when I'm taming it, my aim is to take my time...
Just to make you rush every time we touch
Last night I dreamt of us...
Thinking about how intimate our casual conversations be
At least for me
Pick my brain, you listening to me speak is my weakness
It's the sweetest thing
Next to the sound of your laughter and the song you sing, I mean
No disrespect, I know you'll keep me erect
Not only making you wet, but I'll protect it
Neglecting no part of you
No follicle of hair, mind, body, or the heart of you
Embracing the art of you, I promise, I vow to you
Bow to you, I'll kneel
I know how it feels to bask in a Queen's presence, your essence strong
I swear I still feel you near long after you've gone
I still see you there with nothing on
Soul naked, dressed to perfection yet body nude
Last night... I dreamt of you

Richard "Shake" White

The Interviews (5)

Describe your sexual preference/orientation (ex. Bi, Poly, etc)
I am monogamous
Do you prefer sensuality over physicality? (love making or fucking) explain?
That depends on a lot of things…the person, what I'm feeling at that moment, that situation etc.
What is the easiest way to turn you on / what turns you off?
OMG, that's a lot…turn offs…attitude, conceitedness. I like swagger, the way a man carries himself, is he well spoken…he can talk shit to me as long as he's articulate. The way a man dresses, etc… even in basketball shorts and a t-shirt. Sex appeal is a turn on. Watching how men treat their significant others in public. Small things that a lot of people don't pay attention to
Describe an ideal sexual encounter with you
Hmm… for me that would be, someplace exotic. Example, Fire station (I dated a Fireman) and actually sliding down a pole naked. The way he set it up was a candlelight dinner on a blanket on the floor in the firehouse kitchen. Wine and good conversation…he asked what I liked, what was important to me etc. paying all that attention to me made it personal…that was ideal for me
How do you perform cunnilingus/fellatio? (give tips and tricks)
I don't do anything extra or over the top, I just pay attention to the erogenous areas…the tip, that vein going down the back etc. Slight flickers on the balls etc.
How do you like oral to be performed on you? (give tips and tricks)
Took a long time to find someone who did it right. I'm super sensitive so it's always about the right amount of pressure. I don't want a man to latch on like he's breastfeeding… I prefer a light flicker of the tongue almost like a feather brush
How do you feel about anal? (oral, penetration, toys etc)
My experience with anal wasn't a bad one, but it only took me 1 time to do it to know that I didn't want to do it again. Even

though the guy was attentive and gentle. 1 time was enough, I'll try anything once, it wasn't gratifying for me

How do you feel about bondage? (ever tried it)

It can be sensual, but it can be scary thinking about what a person can do to you….and I'd have to be in control, so that makes it so intriguing. I think everyone should do it.

What are your thoughts on Role Play? What would be an ideal RP?

I like RP and I'm a naughty maid…. I wanna clean up, vacuum and dust in my maid outfit

Favorite position(s) and why?

1st. Reverse Cowgirl. Remember, I like being in control. I have a swing, don't judge me lol. And also, being picked up and eaten out…. that's my absolute favorite. After that, you can't go back to regular sex, you're ruined, lol

What is so special about sexual intercourse with you?

The entire experience… I feel like it's about pleasuring the partner more than yourself. It's tantalizing tantric sex.

Masturbation: How often, what do you do/use?

In college I had the removeable showerhead, then graduated to a BOB…recently I tried the Rose and it's amazing. I masturbate but I really prefer a person cause the toys can't kiss me on my neck and thighs etc

What do you desire to be done to you?

I want to be turned on in every way possible…. Whatever you need to do to do that, I need it. I need the mental, early in the day…send me that text that gets it started. Flirt with me. Say let's have Appetizers… and the appetizers need to be me

What's the wildest thing you ever done or were asked to do sexually?

I was giving a hand job and had researched the basket weave, where you weave your fingers together around the shaft. There was that…also on the balcony, my legs between the bars omg, that was wild, the thought of me falling and breaking my neck!!!

What are your thoughts on 3-somes/orgies?

Richard "Shake" White

Not opposed to a 3 some if it's me and 2 guys, but I don't want to be with another woman. I've attended an orgy before but it wasn't my thing. If I was going to do an orgy I wouldn't go with someone that I was intimately attached to

What do you think about casual sex between acquaintances/friends?

For me I would say, Yes, but that friend has to understand that it's just sex. I don't want to wake up tomorrow and have 50,000 texts talking about I felt something. They have to be able to handle that

What signs do you give off to let someone know that 'they can get it'?

The way I look at you, I would probably subtly touch you in passing, circle back a couple times, staring at you while biting my lip

How would you like to be asked/propositioned for a sexual encounter?

He can say something quirky to catch my attention, shoot your shot. If I'm feeling you, I'm feeling you. Tell me you want some SALT (sex at lunch time)

How much does size matter to you? (Total Body ie stomach, breast, booty, lips, penis, clit etc.)

When I was younger and didn't know anything, that was a thing… Size has nothing to do with how a man treats you and makes you feel. And when he makes you feel sexy and special and desirable, you're in there. A lot of women miss their blessing that way

Bonus: What is your advice that wasn't covered in the questions asked?

Don't compare us to other women, each of us is an individual. Treat us in that manner, just because your ex didn't like something doesn't mean that your next won't. Like eating Oreos, some like to be dunked and some don't.

Describe your sexual preference/orientation (ex. Bi, Poly, etc)

Heterosexual, I prefer to be strictly dickly

Do you prefer sensuality over physicality? (love making or fucking) explain?

It depends on the moment and the mood. I can be loving the intimacy and then all of a sudden, I want to be manhandled. I don't have a preference; I prefer the mood. I'm spontaneous

What is the easiest way to turn you on / what turns you off?

My man looking good is an automatic turn on. The way he looks at me, a certain way, or he's naked…instant turn on. Turn offs are someone being too aggressive, odors, not knowing my body, someone not being versatile in the bedroom. If you're set in your ways and don't want to try things, that's a turn off. Mental Stimulation is a turn on, talking shit and flirting all day…such a turn on

Describe an ideal sexual encounter with you

Nothing's going to be ideal… 1 moment we could be making love, he's kissing me perfectly etc, then it may be like, I want him to bend me over and smack my ass. Role Play, that's it, go with the flow, pull my hair!

How do you perform cunnilingus/fellatio? (give tips and tricks)

You have to enjoy giving head, learn his body, know the parts of his dick, educate yourself. No teeth! Take your time, lick it slow, flick your tongue, make sure it's wet, no man wants a dry mouth. The wetter the better. And your hand technique has to be on point. Lick every part of your man, shaft, tips, balls, etc. I take my time, and make sure I use the right amount of saliva, hand technique, all of that. Practice makes perfect!

How do you like oral to be performed on you? (give tips and tricks)

I believe the same way that I perform. I would like it slow, a lot of focus on the clit. I also like being fingered while my pussy is

90

being eaten. 2 fingers and maneuvering the tongue, slowly. Slow and steady wins the race.

How do you feel about anal? (oral, penetration, toys etc)

I'm not a fan though I've done it a few times. You have to be extremely clean, comfortable and well lubed. I never actually, fully enjoyed it. It took too much of a process to make sure you're clean enough, and the initial pain…. "Ooooweee"

How do you feel about bondage? (ever tried it)

Oh, I love it! That is just sexy, on some 50 Shades of Grey type of thing. Tie me up, blind fold me, swings… do it up, let's have fun.

What are your thoughts on Role Play? What would be an ideal RP?

I love role play, especially when you go someplace, and your man is there and y'all act like you don't know each other and start flirting. Then he takes me home and haves at it. Or the French Maid, Teacher outfits etc. If he wants to cheat, he's gonna cheat with me.

Favorite position(s) and why?

Preference from the back, because I can get it deep as hell, he can smack my ass, go slow or fast, I can back it up if I want to. He can pull my hair, whisper in my ear whatever. I can be punished if I'm being bad! Yes, Doggy style for me.

What is so special about sexual intercourse with you?

I am fun, I can make you do things that your body has never done before. With me, you're not getting someone who wants to lay there. I'm going to make sure that you are pleased. When you're in me, I'm going to make sure that you have the time of your life. I will talk dirty, tell you you're weak etc. And it won't be just 1 time, we're pulling all-nighters. You're getting the full package with me.

Masturbation: How often, what do you do/use?

For me, penetration is the best. Usually, I use the Bullet on the clit. For me plastic isn't my thing, especially when you have a man. The only thing I would do with a toy if it was my choice, is to have it on my clit while my man is inside of me.

What do you desire to be done to you?

I want to be kissed, my eyes to be stared into. I want you to kiss my neck, my back, my nipples, down to my stomach. Lick my legs etc. Take it slow, get me excited, kiss my lips, use your tongue get me wet, fingering me… then when you get me to that moment when I cum…that's when you turn me over and tear me up. Tenderize, season, and marinate!

What's the wildest thing you ever done or were asked to do sexually?

Shit, I'm wild already. I've done it all, I'm the type of person that I just want to do it, I'm spontaneous. Anywhere, at work, elevator, etc

What are your thoughts on 3-somes/orgies?

It's been on my bucket list. I kind of selfish, I don't want nobody touching my man, but I don't think it's a bad thing for people who want to do it. I have done it when I was younger though.

Have you ever participated in a 3-some/orgy? How was it? Would you do it again?

Yes, when I was younger. I wouldn't do it again because it was more of a traumatic thing that had to do with abuse.

What could be improved about your 3-some/orgy experience?

I wouldn't do it again because it was more of a traumatic thing that had to do with abuse.

What do you think about casual sex between acquaintances/friends?

Casual sex, I don't see a problem with it. But when it's continuous, someone is going to catch feelings. Then it turns into 1 reaping all the benefits and 1 left wanting more.

What signs do you give off to let someone know that 'they can get it'?

My eyes give it away every time. I can look at you, bite my lip… I may text you and tell you, but the way I look at you, you're gonna know. Just read my eyes.

How would you like to be asked/propositioned for a sexual encounter?

We just have to have that energy. Don't ask me, I want to know, just by being around you. There's no asking me, it should just flow naturally. You're not going to need to ask, you'll know. Everything will let you know, my body language, my eyes, our conversation etc. When you can read me and actually know what I want without talking about sex… that's what gets my panties off. It has to happen organically. Energy is energy.

How much does size matter to you? (Total Body ie stomach, breast, booty, lips, penis, clit etc.)

For me, I like a guy that can handle me. I don't really like a skinny dude. It's not really about size, I just need a man that can handle and manhandle me. I like a man that takes care of himself, I want visual appeal. Girls that say they want a 10-inch dick are lying. You can't take that pounding every day. But I also don't need you to be 3 or 4 inches. I'm fine with an average build guy but take care of yourself.

Bonus: What is your advice that wasn't covered in the questions asked?

Just be mentally stimulating, we have to have that chemistry. Otherwise, it's just casual sex.

Women give cues and clues to what they want you to do to her body. Try different things. Stop trying to put all that fruit inside of your women. Our Ph gets messed up really easily. Take it slow guys, don't pound the woman. Learn about the Man or woman's body.

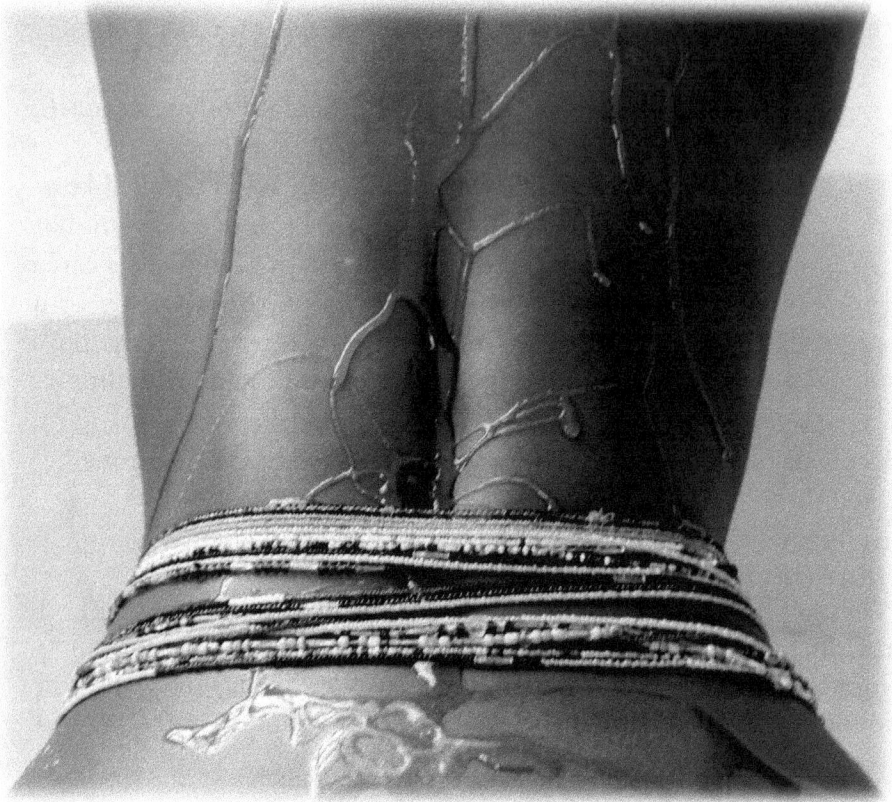

Richard "Shake" White

310brownstreet.com
@310brownstreet

CL!T

Richard "Shake" White

www.ingramcontent.com/pod-product-compliance
Lightning Source LLC
Chambersburg PA
CBHW072207090426
42740CB00012B/2419